D0927004

UNDERSTANDING
THE PATH TO
CITIZENSHIP

BY KREMENA SPENGLER

SE⚙U
ENCE

AMICUS | AMICUS INK

Sequence is published by Amicus and Amicus Ink
P.O. Box 1329, Mankato, MN 56002
www.amicuspublishing.us

Library of Congress Cataloging-in-Publication Data
Names: Spengler, Kremena, author.
Title: Understanding the path to citizenship / by Kremena Spengler.
Description: Mankato, Minnesota : Amicus, [2020] | Series: Sequence American
  government | Audience: Grades: K to 3. | Includes bibliographical
  references and index.
Identifiers: LCCN 2018049811 (print) | LCCN 2018061250 (ebook) |
  ISBN 9781681517520 (pdf) | ISBN 9781681516707 (library binding) |
  ISBN 9781681524566 (paperback)
Subjects: LCSH: Citizenship–United States–Juvenile literature. |
  Immigrants–United States–Juvenile literature.
Classification: LCC JK1759 (ebook) | LCC JK1759 .S66 2020 (print) | DDC
  323.6/20973–dc23
LC record available at https://lccn.loc.gov/2018049811

Editor: Alissa Thielges
Designer: Veronica Scott
Photo Researcher: Holly Young

Photo Credits: Getty/Aaron MCcoy cover; iStock/bowdenimages 5; Getty/Juanmonino
6-7; iStock/FatCamera 8; Shutterstock/nito 11; AP/Jose Luis Magana 12-13;
Shutterstock/franz12 15; Alamy/Ken Hawkins 16; Getty/John Moore 19; Shutterstock/
Kristi Blokhin 20; Getty/The Washington Post 22-23; Getty/John Moore 24; Newscom/
Paul Hennessy, Polaris 27; Getty/Tetra Images 28

Printed in the United States of America

HC 10 9 8 7 6 5 4 3 2
PB 10 9 8 7 6 5 4 3 2 1

One Country, Many Faces

Do you wonder why your friends look different from each other? Their eyes, hair, and skin vary. Some speak only English. Some can speak another language. This is for a reason. American families have come from all over the world. Freedom and opportunities draw people to the United States.

The U.S. is a very **diverse** country.

LOADING...LOADING...LOADING...

Many people come to the United States to find a better life.

People who move to a new country are called **immigrants**. In the United States, immigrants can say what they think. They can work to make their lives better.

But some rights are only for U.S. **citizens**. Only citizens can vote. Only citizens can run for office. Many immigrants want to be citizens.

LOADING...LOADING...LOADING...

A woman applies for a green card.

LOADING...LOADING...LOADING...

Paths to Citizenship

Were you born in the United States? If so, you are a citizen already. By law, you are a **citizen by birth**. If at least one of your parents is a citizen, you are also a citizen.

Immigrants can become citizens. This is called **naturalization**. But first, you need permission to live in the United States. This is known as a **green card**.

It is not easy to get a green card. One way is to marry a U.S. citizen. Or, a citizen can request green cards for family members in other countries. Some cards are saved for **refugees** who are fleeing their country. Skilled workers also get special green cards. These workers excel at their work.

A green card is an ID for immigrants. It lets them live and work in the U.S.

Find out how to get a green card.

YEAR 1 LOADING... LOADING...

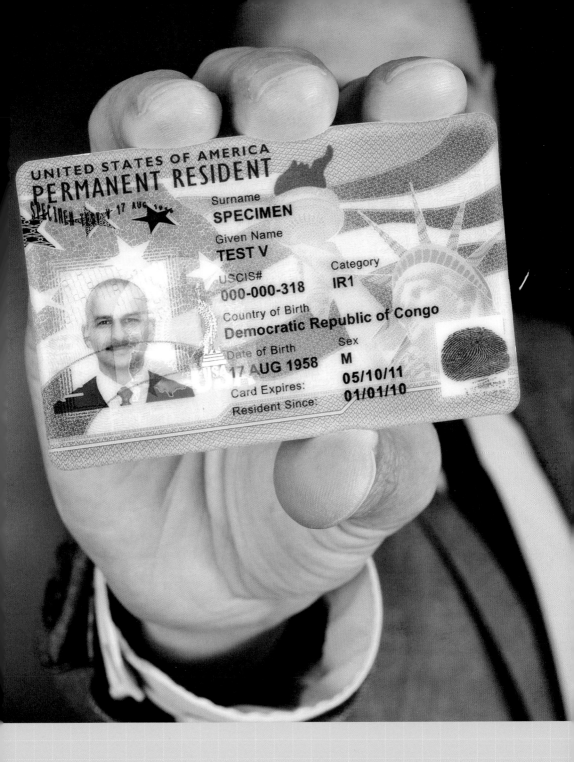

Find out how to get
a green card.

YEAR 1 ⟶

ING . . . LOADING . . .

Enter the green
card lottery.

One unusual way to get a green card is in a lottery. This is a random drawing. It gives people from all over the world a chance to win a green card. People put their names in. Each year, 50,000 names are drawn. But even if a person wins, the green card is not theirs for sure.

Young immigrants file for permission to stay in the United States.

A background check is needed to get a green card. This checks for any crimes committed. Your fingerprints are taken. You also must prove you have at least a high school education. Even health records and X-rays are needed! The government will also interview you before the card is granted.

Fingerprints are part of the required background check for a green card.

Find out how to get a green card.

Get a background check; collect education and health records.

YEAR 1 ⟶ YEAR 2

LOADING . . .

Enter the green card lottery.

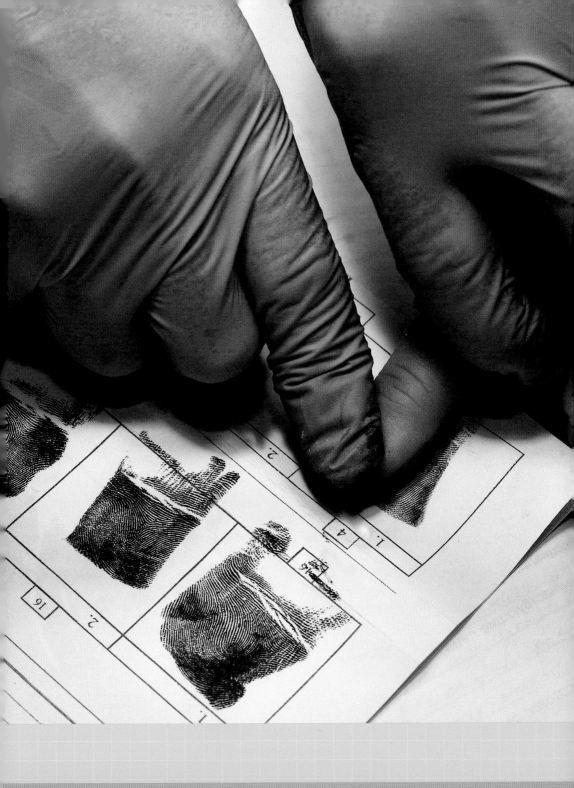

LOADING..LOADING..LOADING...

An immigrant family moves into a new home. They are ready to start a new life in the United States.

Find out how to get a green card.

Get a background check; collect education and health records.

YEAR 1

YEAR 2

Enter the green card lottery.

Live lawfully as a permanent resident for five years.

The Application

Finally, a green card! It makes you a **permanent resident**. You can move in and look for a job. Make sure to obey the laws! You can't become a citizen if you commit a crime. There are other rules to follow, too. For example, you can't leave the country for more than six months in a row. After five years, you can apply to be a citizen.

The citizen application is long. There are many questions on the form. It tells a lot about you. A second set of fingerprints and a photo are taken. These are used to make sure that people are who they say they are. They are also used to do a more in-depth background check.

A man looks through a citizen application form.

Find out how to get a green card.

Get a background check; collect education and health records.

Apply to become a citizen.

YEAR 1 ——————————→ YEAR 2 ——————————→ YEAR 7

Enter the green card lottery.

Live lawfully as a permanent resident for five years.

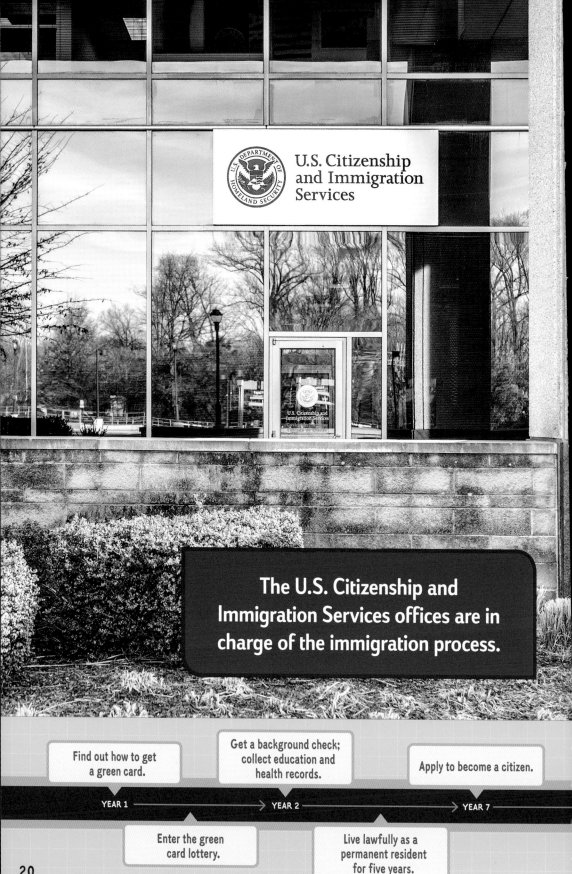

The U.S. Citizenship and Immigration Services offices are in charge of the immigration process.

Find out how to get a green card.

Get a background check; collect education and health records.

Apply to become a citizen.

YEAR 1

YEAR 2

YEAR 7

Enter the green card lottery.

Live lawfully as a permanent resident for five years.

The Interview

Next is the interview. A date and time is set. Before the interview, you'll want to prepare for the tests. The tests are on the English language and U.S. **civics**. It is important to study for them. A study booklet is available.

At the interview, an officer checks the answers on your application. The officer may also ask you more questions about yourself.

LOADING...LOADING...

Prepare and show up for the interview.

In the interview, you must show you know English. The officer asks you to read and write sentences. They listen to you speak.

The civics test follows. There are 100 questions. But the officer will only ask you ten. A person must answer six questions correctly to pass. Most of the questions are about U.S. history and government.

A woman uses a study guide to prepare for the tests.

Find out how to get a green card.

Get a background check; collect education and health records.

Apply to become a citizen.

YEAR 1

YEAR 2

YEAR 7

Enter the green card lottery.

Live lawfully as a permanent resident for five years.

The Federalist papers worked, and soon the Constitution was adopted.

PUBLIUS

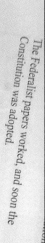

http://covers.feedbooks.net/book/2674.jpg?size=la rge&t=1376747641

After the Constitutional Convention, George Washington became the first president.

George Washington is the Father of Our Country.

George Washington is also on the one dollar bill.

Computer Activity:
http://s3.amazonaws.com/mtv-main-assets/files/callouts/gilbert-stuart-george-2.jpg

• • Visit the CARECEN DC Quia page and try these activities.

• American History: the 1700s
Smithsonian Test Preparation website > Start Learning > Writing

• the Constitution

Take the English and U.S. civics tests.

ING . . . LOADING . . .

Prepare and show up for the interview.

BENEFITS OF CITIZENSHIP

| Find out how to get a green card. | Get a background check; collect education and health records. | Apply to become a citizen. |

YEAR 1 → YEAR 2 → YEAR 7

| Enter the green card lottery. | Live lawfully as a permanent resident for five years. |

When the interview is over, the officer tells you how you did. If you fail a test, you must retake it.

You may be told you do not get to be a citizen. This happens when you do not meet all requirements. You may be asked for more information. You have 12 weeks to submit it.

This woman gets help with her citizen application.

Take the English and U.S. civics tests.

LOADING . . .

Prepare and show up for the interview.

Submit more information to support your case, if needed.

New Citizens

If you pass, you will be invited to a ceremony. It is often in a special, historic place. You and other immigrants will take an **oath** before a judge. It is a promise to support the United States. You also promise to obey the Constitution. You are now a citizen!

New citizens take the oath to support the United States.

Find out how to get a green card.

Get a background check; collect education and health records.

Apply to become a citizen.

YEAR 1 → YEAR 2 → YEAR 7

Enter the green card lottery.

Live lawfully as a permanent resident for five years.

Take the English and
U.S. civics tests.

Attend a ceremony
and take an oath.

→ YEAR 8

Prepare and show up
for the interview.

Submit more information
to support your case,
if needed.

Voting in an election is a citizen's right.

Find out how to get a green card.

Get a background check; collect education and health records.

Apply to become a citizen.

YEAR 1 ——————————————→ YEAR 2 ———————————→ YEAR 7

Enter the green card lottery.

Live lawfully as a permanent resident for five years.

Citizens enjoy many rights. They can vote in elections. They can help their families become citizens. In turn, citizens are responsible for serving the United States. They may be called to serve in the military or on a jury. Becoming a citizen is not an easy process. But citizens can enjoy the benefits for the rest of their lives.

Take the English and U.S. civics tests.

Attend a ceremony and take an oath.

YEAR 8

Prepare and show up for the interview.

Submit more information to support your case, if needed.

Register to vote.

Glossary

citizen A member of a country who has all the rights and responsibilities the country offers.

citizen by birth In the United States, a person born in the country or a person born to a parent who is a U.S. citizen.

civics The study of the rights and duties of citizens.

diverse Having a lot of variety; very different.

green card An identification card that lets immigrants live and work permanently in the United States.

immigrant A person who moves to a new country.

naturalization The process to become a U.S. citizen.

oath A serious, formal promise.

permanent resident A person who can live and work in the United States but is not a citizen.

refugee A person who is running from war, persecution, or injustice in his or her country.

Read More

Kenney, Karen. *Civic Responsibilities*. Vero Beach, Fla.: Rourke Educational Media, 2015.

Poehlmann, Tristan. *12 Immigrants Who Made American Technology Great*. A Nation of Immigrants. North Mankato, Minn.: 12 Story Library, 2019.

Small, Cathleen. *Becoming a U.S. Citizen*. New York: Lucent Press, 2018.

Websites

Ducksters | Becoming a US Citizen
https://www.ducksters.com/history/us_government/becoming_a_us_citizen.php

iCivics | Immigration Nation Game
https://www.icivics.org/node/4474

USCIS — Learn About Naturalization
https://www.uscis.gov/citizenship/learners/learn-about-naturalization

Index

About the Author

Kremena Spengler is an editor and writer in New Ulm, Minnesota. She immigrated to the United States from Bulgaria, and English is her third language. She has written many books for kids on topics ranging from geography and history to famous people and inventions. She loves reading, world travel, chocolate, and running.